Tecumseh

by

Deborah Stone

Director of Education
Marjorie L. Kelley, Ed.D.

Executive Editor
Corinn Codye Scott

Illustrator
James Balkovek

History Consultant
Bruce Glasrud, Ph.D.
Professor of American History
California State University, Hayward

QUERCUS
A Division of Globe Book Company
Englewood Cliffs, New Jersey

Printed in the United States of America
10 9 8 7 6 5 4 3
ISBN 1-55555-036-3

Contents

The two brothers, Tecumseh and the Prophet, call upon all Indian tribes to join as one people.

The Shawnee Talk of War

Tecumseh sat on the dirt floor of the big council house. Around the fire with him were other Shawnee men and women. They were holding a council.

In this council, the Shawnee tried to decide what to do. They would not leave the council house until everyone agreed. Some Shawnee wanted to give the white settlers land. They thought that only then would the white settlers let them alone. Others thought fighting the whites was the only way to make them leave.

The Shawnee war chief, Little Turtle, stood up to speak. In 1790, Little Turtle led the Shawnee in a fight against the whites. They had pushed the whites out of Ohio. Now the year was 1794. The whites wanted to take back Ohio from the Indians. But Little Turtle was afraid of the whites.

"The whites will not stop killing our people," Little Turtle said. He was tired of fighting. "We must give them the land they want. Then they will let us alone."

The Shawnee listened quietly. The women chiefs were also there. Their job was to present a case for peace.

Tecumseh's sister was one of them. She rose to speak.

"Already, the whites have begun to march," she said. "There are many more white soldiers than braves. I do not want to see any more Shawnee die."

Tecumseh wanted to speak. But no one would listen to him yet. Tecumseh was 26 years old. Even though he was known as a brave fighter, he was still too young to speak in council.

Tecumseh hated the whites. They had killed his father and a brother. Tecumseh's sister had raised him.

Tecumseh believed the Shawnee had to fight. For years Tecumseh had led attacks against the settlers. It seemed that no matter how much Indian land the settlers got, they wanted more.

Tecumseh looked over at Blue Jacket. Blue Jacket was like a father to Tecumseh. He was the one who taught Tecumseh how to fight. There was gray in Blue Jacket's hair. Blue Jacket stood and turned to Little Turtle.

"Your heart has grown cold, old man," Blue Jacket said to Little Turtle. His voice was fierce. "I have stood by your side in the past. Now, I will fight without you. White people are hungry for our land. They kill our game and burn our crops. Our people have no food to eat."

The settlers believed they had won Ohio from Great Britain by winning the Revolutionary War. The American government had to spend a lot of money to fight the

Revolutionary War. Now the government needed more money. One way to get it was to sell land in Ohio to white settlers.

The settlers bought land for farming and moved to Ohio. About 10,000 settlers came every year. They traveled over bad roads in wagons packed with everything they owned. The trip was very hard.

But the settlers found Indians on land they thought they owned. They feared the Indians. They did not know the Shawnee loved the land, too.

The whites did not plan to lose this fight against the Shawnee. They picked General "Mad" Anthony Wayne to lead their army. A man who knew about fighting Indians, Wayne trained his army well.

The Shawnee council went on all night. Everyone had a chance to speak. In the end, the Shawnee decided to go on the warpath. They named Blue Jacket as their new war chief.

The Battle of the Fallen Timbers

The Shawnee watched General Wayne's army come closer and closer. Wayne marched very slowly toward Shawnee land. Along his way, he stopped to build big forts.

The forts were made of logs the soldiers cut down in the forest. The settlers were glad to see the forts go up. When the Indians attacked, whole families went inside the forts to hide.

Blue Jacket picked Tecumseh to watch Wayne's army. Tecumseh traveled quietly through the forest, watching every move the white army made. Tecumseh stood almost six feet tall, but he seemed taller. He was very strong. Tecumseh dressed in plain deerskin shirt and leggings, refusing to wear white men's clothes. Through his nose he wore a silver ring. He also had a white eagle feather in his long, black hair.

Tecumseh rode back to Blue Jacket and told him what he had seen. Blue Jacket listened carefully and decided to attack. If the Shawnee did not move soon, even more soldiers might join General Wayne. Already there were more whites than Shawnee by two to one.

So Blue Jacket sent his braves out to fight. He had them hide behind giant trees that blew down in a big storm. That is why this fight came to be called the Battle of Fallen Timbers.

Tecumseh led a small party of braves into thick brush. They surprised the soldiers on the white army's front line.

"Fight hard," Tecumseh called out. "We must not give one inch." The whites fired without letting up. The Shawnee could hardly poke their heads out from behind the trees.

Then Tecumseh's gun began to stick. He threw it away and continued to fight hand to hand.

"Come, men. I will show you how to fight these Long Knives," he shouted. (The Indians called white people Long Knives.) "If I had a gun, I would send these whites running."

"Take this," called Tecumseh's brother. He threw over a small gun used to hunt birds. Suddenly Tecumseh's brother fell down dead with a bullet in his back.

Tecumseh went on fighting. Tecumseh was angry. His black eyes flashed. Another person in his family was dead at the hands of the whites.

Tecumseh's braves battled even harder because he was with them. But the Indians didn't stand a chance. The white army had more guns, men, and training. They attacked on horseback and with cannon—very big guns. The Shawnee had only small guns, and bows and arrows.

Knowing the fight was over, the braves moved quietly back through the forest. They didn't even have time to take their dead with them. In the rear of the army, Tecumseh found white soldiers with a horse-pulled cannon. The Indians chased the whites away and cut the horses free. Then they rode away before the soldiers could catch up with them.

Tecumseh's Plan for All Indians

The Shawnee had lost the battle. They left their village and moved farther away from the whites. In their new village, the Shawnee built wigwams of poles woven around with bark. The women planted new fields of corn, beans, and squash.

Tecumseh thought about what the Indians could do to stop the whites. He thought he saw the problem. There were so many different tribes. Each tribe spoke a different language and had different ways. Each tribe had a different chief. On the other hand, the whites were united. They all spoke the same language. One chief ruled them all.

The Indians had to learn to work together as one group, Tecumseh decided.

After the battle, Wayne went through Ohio burning Indian fields and villages. Then Wayne called the chiefs to a great peace council. Blue Jacket and Little Turtle came to this council. But Tecumseh was not invited. Wayne brought food and lots of whiskey, which the Indians called firewater.

The Indians drank firewater for two weeks. Then Wayne presented the chiefs with a piece of paper. He told them to sign it. Twelve tribes signed this piece of paper, known as the Greenville Treaty. It gave all of Ohio to the settlers.

In return, the Indians got about $20,000 for all that land. The whites also wrote a promise into the treaty. They promised never to settle on any land the Indians still owned.

After the council, Blue Jacket told Tecumseh about the treaty. Tecumseh grew angry. His proud, dark eyes burned.

"What chiefs sell our land for a few barrels of firewater? Has your heart grown cold too, old man?" Tecumseh asked.

Blue Jacket looked sad. He no longer thought the white man could be stopped. "The white fathers promise this land will always be ours," Blue Jacket said.

Tecumseh's eyes flashed. "The white man lies," he said. "The white man has broken every treaty he has made with us. Do you think he will suddenly change?

"Our land will not be safe until the white man is gone," said Tecumseh. "I will not rest my feet until all Indians join together as one people. Only then can we fight the white man."

Loud Mouth, the Prophet

In the following years, the Shawnee often called on Tecumseh for help. He stood up for his people's rights. The Shawnee loved Tecumseh. They were very proud of him. Tecumseh was a good hunter who always shared his meat. And he never drank firewater.

Tecumseh's youngest brother lived in the same village as Tecumseh. This brother's name was Loud Mouth. Loud Mouth had only one eye, so he could not hunt. He had hurt the other eye while shooting an arrow that broke in half.

Loud Mouth made Tecumseh angry. For one thing, Loud Mouth drank too much firewater. His family never had any food. Most Shawnee agreed with Tecumseh that Loud Mouth was good for nothing. But Tecumseh made sure that Loud Mouth and his family had food to eat.

One day, Loud Mouth sat in front of his fire. He lit his pipe from the fire, then he fell over. His wife tried to wake him, but could not. Thinking that Loud Mouth was dead, his wife washed his body. Everyone cried and sang songs over him. Outside, his neighbors made a hole in the ground.

They lined it with wood and bark and got ready to bury Loud Mouth.

Suddenly, Loud Mouth sat up. He told everyone he had been to the spirit world.

"In the spirit world, the Shawnee have plenty of game and fish to eat. They plant fields of corn and beans. Our people play and hunt there as they did before the white man came."

When Loud Mouth finished telling his story, he began to shake. He promised never to drink firewater again. Tecumseh did not believe Loud Mouth's words. But Loud Mouth never did touch a drop of firewater again.

Loud Mouth told everyone about his trips to the spirit world. The Shawnee began to call Loud Mouth the Prophet. More Shawnee came to listen to him. Even Indians from other tribes heard about the Prophet and came to hear him.

After one of these trips, Loud Mouth (the Prophet) told the Indians that the Great Spirit had spoken to him. "It is not easy to please the Great Spirit," said the Prophet. "To do so, you must return to the ways of your fathers' fathers. The white people have taken away our land. But the Great Spirit made this land for us. If you do what I tell you, the whites will go back over the ocean. Our land will be returned to us."

Tecumseh and the Prophet Lead the Shawnee

The two brothers, Tecumseh and the Prophet, worked together. The Prophet talked to the Indians about returning to the ways of their fathers. Tecumseh spoke, too. He talked about the land. It could not be sold, Tecumseh said, any more than air or water could be sold.

The white man's coming had changed the Indians' lives. Many tribes had big problems with whiskey. Whites often used firewater instead of money to buy things. Sometimes, whole villages of Indians got so drunk they sold everything to the whites. They even sold the land they sat on.

Before the white man came, Indians shared everything with each other. But now they refused to share with those in want. The Prophet saw that these things had to change.

After the Prophet spoke, the Indians sang and danced. They were happy. But the whites living near this village grew frightened. There were too many Indians in one place. The settlers thought the Indians planned war.

The settlers who lived in Ohio went to Governor William Henry Harrison. Harrison had been a soldier in General

Wayne's army during the Battle of Fallen Timbers. Now he was the governor of the land in the West. His job was to make sure the Indians and settlers got along together. He also had orders from the American president to buy land from the Indians.

The settlers complained to Harrison about the many Indians in the village. Harrison began to worry about all the Indians going to hear the Prophet. He also thought the Indians might plan to attack the settlers.

Governor Harrison decided to write a letter to the Indians. He wanted to turn them away from their Prophet.

"Ask this Prophet to make the sky darken or the rivers change course. If he does these things, then you may believe him," the governor's letter said.

But the Prophet seemed to know more than the governor. One bright day, he called the village people together.

"My people," he told them, "I will cause the sun to darken. Then you will know that the Great Spirit speaks through me." He waited for the voices to die down. Then he slowly raised his arms and pointed at the sun.

"My Father, I call upon you to make the sun dark."

At that very moment, the sun grew dark. Everyone cried out in fear.

The Prophet walked among his people. "Did I not speak the truth?" he asked them. The Indians begged him to bring

16

the sun back.

The Prophet asked the Great Spirit to return the sun's bright face. The shadow passed from the sun.

Many believe the Prophet found out about this eclipse of the sun from settlers. But no one is sure how, or even if, the Prophet knew about the eclipse.

The story flew like fire to all the villages. Even more Indians came to hear the Prophet. The governor's plan had backfired.

Prophet's Town

Governor Harrison had to so something. The settlers needed more land. They had come from far away. Women packed up wagons, putting in clothing and seeds for their new gardens. Whole families left their homes behind.

There wasn't enough food or land for everyone. Tecumseh moved his village farther away from the settlers. He picked a place on the Tippecanoe River with plenty of good soil. The Shawnee women could plant their crops. There would be plenty of corn and beans for everyone who came to hear the Prophet. There was still game for the men to hunt.

Best of all, whites could make no claim to the land here. It had always belonged to the Indians. An Indian village had always stood on this spot.

This new village was named Prophet's Town. After building the village, Tecumseh began to travel. He went from tribe to tribe. At each village, Tecumseh called a council of all the men and women. He told them that Indians must stop fighting each other. To stop whites from taking all their land, Indians had to join as one people. The word for this joining together is confederation. Only by uniting in a confederation of tribes, Tecumseh said, could Indians keep their land.

Many tribes were interested in Tecumseh's idea. They agreed to send braves to Tecumseh. But some tribes did not want to listen. To them, other Indians—not whites—were the enemy. These tribes had always warred with each other. They could not imagine fighting anyone else. Still other tribes were used to white people. They did not hate whites as Tecumseh did.

Tecumseh traveled for four years. He went to every Indian tribe he could. He went in person to each tribe, by horse, by boat, or on foot.

Governor Harrison's soldiers told him about all the tribes joining Tecumseh. Harrison thought too many tribes were listening to Tecumseh. Tecumseh had talked many chiefs out of selling their land to the Americans.

Harrison also feared that Great Britain would get the Indians over to their side. Though Great Britain lost the Revolutionary War, they still wanted to make trouble for America. They gave the Indians guns to fight with.

Governor Harrison decided to act. He waited for Tecumseh to leave Prophet's Town on a trip. Then Harrison got all the friendly chiefs together at a council. One of these chiefs was Little Turtle.

The Indians drank firewater for many days. Then Harrison talked the chiefs into signing another treaty. This treaty, called the Treaty of Fort Wayne, was signed in 1809. It sold 3,000,000 acres to the Americans. Harrison paid the chiefs only $10,000 for land worth $6,000,000 at that time.

"Do Not Sell Our Land!"

When Tecumseh heard about Harrison's new treaty, he became angrier than ever. He knew Harrison had waited for him to leave to make the treaty.

Tecumseh was even angrier at the chiefs who sold the land. He called his own council, making sure the women came too. The women did not like it when land they grew corn and beans on was sold.

"These chiefs care only about money they get from the Long Knives. Together we own this land," Tecumseh said. "A few men cannot sell what belongs to all."

Tecumseh's sister stood up. "You must go to Governor Harrison," she said. "You tell him these chiefs don't speak for all our people. Then the governor will return the land to us."

"You speak well, sister. I will go," Tecumseh said. "Who will come with me?"

Many Shawnee went with him, among them Tecumseh's sister. She wore a new deerskin dress. The Indians wore new deerskin leggings. The braves painted themselves with red paint. Tecumseh wore an eagle feather in his hair.

Governor Harrison waited for the Indians. He put chairs inside for them. But Tecumseh liked to sit out under the sky.

"Houses are made for white men to hold councils in," Tecumseh told Harrison. "Indians hold theirs in the open air."

Then one of Harrison's soldiers went to Tecumseh. He pointed to the house.

"Your father wants you at his side," the soldier said. By "father," the soldier meant Governor Harrison.

Tecumseh looked up with a fierce eye. He raised his strong arms and pointed at the sky. "My father?! The Great Spirit is my father. The earth is my mother. I will sit on her."

Tecumseh sat on the ground, cross-legged. His braves sat near him. The governor went outside and sat by Tecumseh. He held the council where Tecumseh wanted.

Tecumseh began to speak.

"Once the red men were a happy people. But the white man has made us unhappy," Tecumseh said. "There used to be no white men in this land. It belonged to us, the children of the Great Spirit. He placed us on this land to enjoy it."

Then Tecumseh laughed. He looked around at everyone, both Indian and white. They sat silently and listened to his words. No one spoke more beautifully than Tecumseh.

"Sell a country? Why not sell the air? Why not sell the great sea? The Great Spirit made earth and sea for all his children. You talk about giving us money for land. But my people want to save the land. We do not want your money.

"I speak for all my people. I tell you we don't want you on our land. If you come, you are to blame for the trouble you cause."

Harrison replied, "I will tell the Great White Father, the president, your words. But I do not think he will agree."

Tecumseh thought over Governor Harrison's words. Tecumseh knew then the land would not be returned, no matter what he said. Tecumseh turned to leave. But before he left, he said sadly, "Your Great White Father is far away. A war will not hurt him. But you and I will have to fight it out."

Harrison Attacks Prophet's Town

The white settlers were angry. Hadn't they bought this land from the Indians? There were treaties to prove the whites now owned the land. Anyway, there was plenty of land. Why didn't the Indians just go somewhere else?

Both sides thought they were right. Tecumseh could see a war coming. White settlers shot at Indians as if they were animals. So Tecumseh went to ask Harrison to protect the Indians. Tecumseh told Harrison that he had to go on another trip. Tecumseh feared that while he was gone the settlers would attack his village. Harrison promised to look after the Indians at Prophet's Town.

But Harrison secretly thought Tecumseh was going to talk to other tribes about war. He thought Tecumseh was a dangerous man. So Harrison wrote to the American president asking for soldiers. "We must break up Tecumseh and the Prophet's group," Harrison wrote.

Tecumseh was a fine fighter. Harrison did not want to fight Tecumseh. So he waited for Tecumseh to leave. Then he marched on Prophet's Town.

The Prophet watched Harrison's army move closer and closer to Prophet's Town. Though Tecumseh told his brother not to fight, what could the Prophet do? With an army of 1,000 soldiers marching, he could not turn and run. His followers would never stop laughing at him.

The night before the white soldiers attacked, the Prophet called all the braves together.

"My brother Tecumseh has gone to call others to our side," he said. "We must stand and fight. The Great Spirit will protect you from the Long Knives' bullets. You will be safe."

All night the Indians sang and danced and prayed to the Great Spirit. Then, before sunrise, the Prophet sent his braves to attack Harrison's camp. Two braves broke into the camp and shot at sleeping soldiers. The braves wanted to kill Harrison, but two white soldiers killed them first.

When Harrison finally got to the front line, the Indians had broken through. The Indians poured a heavy rain of bullets on the white army. Harrison rode up and down the lines. He called for more soldiers to back them up.

One group of Indians hid in some trees. They fired right into the white soldiers' faces, killing many. But whenever a white soldier died, two more came to take his place.

The Prophet watched the battle from a hill near the village. He prayed to the Great Spirit to protect his braves. But once again the Indians did not have enough men.

The braves saw that the Prophet had lied to them. Many Indians died, even though the Prophet promised they would not. The few braves left fighting turned and ran. The battle ended. This fight is called the Battle of Tippecanoe because it happened on the Tippecanoe River.

Back at the village, the braves shouted at the Prophet. They held sticks over his head and told him they would kill him. Didn't the Prophet say they would not be hurt by the white soldiers' bullets? Yet many braves had been killed by those same bullets. Why had he lied to them?

The Indians feared that Harrison's army would march on the village soon. The Indians got their families and left. They took as much food as they could carry.

When Harrison came, he found one woman too old and sick to travel. He also found guns made by Great Britain. Now Harrison knew the British had helped the Indians. He burned the village to the ground, all except the old woman's wigwam.

News that British guns had been found at Prophet's Town flashed across the West. In 1812, the Americans decided to go to war with Great Britain again.

Tecumseh Returns

Tecumseh continued to travel around the South asking Indian tribes to join his confederation. He had no idea the whites had burned Prophet's Town to the ground.

Few tribes in the South wanted to join together. Some tribes did not like the Shawnee. Others had been on the American side in the Revolutionary War. They liked the Americans.

After six months, Tecumseh had done all he could. He headed sadly back to Prophet's Town. He got excited just thinking about seeing his people again. After weeks of walking through the forest, Tecumseh rounded a bend in the river.

He saw his village, but it looked strange and silent. Something was different. Then, Tecumseh saw the burned wigwams. A few children played outside. Tecumseh saw his sister bending over in a field. He went over to her.

"Sister," Tecumseh said.

She stood up in surprise and put her arms around him.

"Brother, I am sorry for what your eyes will see today," she said. Then she told Tecumseh about the Battle of Tippecanoe. "Some of the men, women, and children have returned. Most have gone back to their own people. They are angry. They no longer believe the Prophet's words."

Tecumseh could not believe his eyes or his ears. He went right to the Prophet and asked him what had happened.

The Prophet was afraid. He told Tecumseh the Long Knives had attacked with 1,000 soldiers.

"Didn't I tell you not to fight if they marched?" Tecumseh shouted.

"Was I supposed to run away?" the Prophet asked. "Your braves did not fight well," he said. "They are to blame."

Tecumseh pulled his brother by the hair. He wanted to kill him. For four years Tecumseh had worked to bring the Indians together. Now all his hard work counted for nothing. Instead of killing his brother, Tecumseh sent him away.

Then Tecumseh began all over. He had not had time to bring the tribes together to fight the Americans. Now America and Great Britain were at war. Tecumseh would go to war against the Americans, too. He would try again to get the tribes to unite. This time, he would use British guns and soldiers to help.

Tecumseh's Last Battle

After the Battle of Tippecanoe, Tecumseh built a new wigwam in Prophet's Town. He sent men to all the tribes he had ever visited. His men told these tribes that America and Britain had gone to war. The only way to push the Americans back was to fight on Great Britain's side.

During the next two years, 3,000 Indians joined Tecumseh. They picked him as their war chief.

The American government became alarmed by the number of braves joining Tecumseh. Now they wanted Tecumseh fighting on their side. They were sorry about the Battle of Tippecanoe.

So the Americans invited Tecumseh to a peace council. Tecumseh came to this council with many of his braves. But he broke the peace pipe the Americans passed around.

"Does this mean you are at war with us?" the Americans wanted to know.

"I do not know what I will do with my men," Tecumseh answered. "But I will never again have such a chance to fight the Long Knives."

With help from Great Britain, Tecumseh's braves won several battles. Tecumseh led his men fearlessly. Then the British general was killed. The next general was not as brave as the first. The Indians and the British began to lose the war.

Indians from other tribes began to leave Tecumseh's side. Some tribes just wanted to be on the winning side. Other tribes thought the war was over already.

But Tecumseh kept on fighting to the very end. His last battle was against his old enemy, William Henry Harrison. No longer governor, Harrison now led the large American army. He attacked Tecumseh's camp. The British soldiers in Tecumseh's camp ran away after only five minutes of fighting.

Tecumseh watched the British soldiers run. With only a few hundred braves left, Tecumseh stood against Harrison's army. Tecumseh fell with a bullet in his heart. Within 30 minutes, the fighting stopped. With their chief dead, Tecumseh's braves lost their will to fight.

The night after the battle, a group of Tecumseh's braves came to the battlefield to look for their chief's body. They looked everywhere. When the braves found Tecumseh's body, they carried it several miles away and buried it in the forest.

Ending Note

Tecumseh's dream of a confederation of Indian tribes died with him. After many years, the settlers pushed the Indians onto small pieces of land called reservations. The whites gave the Indians the worst land for their reservations. Many Indian tribes still live on these reservations. Most are very poor.

No one has ever found the spot where Tecumseh was buried. The Prophet died on the Shawnee reservation, a broken man, in 1836.

During his years in the West, Harrison bought 48,000,000 acres, all of Ohio and Indiana, from the Indians. William Henry Harrison became president in 1841, 30 years after the Battle of Tippecanoe.

Places in the Life of Tecumseh (1768–1813)